A Lion
Called Christian

A Lion
Called Christian

Anthony Bourke and John Rendall

Doubleday & Company, Inc.
Garden City, New York
1972

To our families, who
never met Christian

Acknowledgements

We want to thank these people for making Christian's life with us in England both possible and happy, and for helping to "return" him to where he belonged: Roy Hazle and Sandy Lloyd at Harrods; Jenny Taylor, Joe Harding, John Barnardiston and Kay Dew at Sophisto-Cat; the World's End; The Reverend H. R. and Mrs. Williamson and Joan and Rod Thomas at the Moravian Close; Unity Bevis and Amelia Nathan, Christian's best friends; Jeremy Faull for his help and advice; Bill and Virginia Travers for making it all possible; James Hill for the filming; Monty and Hilary Ruben for their marvellous hospitality in Nairobi; Terence Adamson for his work at Garissa; and George Adamson for what he is doing for Christian and the other lions.

We would also like to thank, for helping with this book, our patient editor Adrian House, Toni Rendall, Amanda Barrett, and Derek Cattani for his photographs in England and Kenya.

Foreword by George Adamson

In April 1970, I received a letter from London from my friend Bill Travers, telling me about "Christian" a fifth generation English lion and asking whether I would be prepared to take him over and rehabilitate him back to the wild of his forebears. The idea appealed to me greatly, not only because it would save Christian from a life-time of captivity, but also because it would be, in all probability the first time an English lion had been returned to the life for which he was created.

I felt confident that his inherited knowledge and instincts would soon assert themselves, given the chance, and in spite of his breeding. I must admit that I did not feel the same confidence about his two owners, when I heard that they would accompany Christian and stay a few weeks at my camp. I was led to believe they were very "mod" with long hair and exotic clothing. My first sight at Nairobi Airport of pink bell-bottomed trousers and flowing locks did nothing to dispel my misgivings. But Ace and John soon restored my faith in the modern generation. Immediately, I sensed the bond of deep affection and trust between them and Christian. I know from experience how hard it must have been for them to leave Christian to face the inevitable dangers and hardships of a lion in the wild.

At the time of writing, Christian is nearly two years old. He is as much at home in this wilderness as if he had been born here. Apart from initial toughening-up, he required no training. Always the wonderful store house of inherited knowledge has shown him the way.

GEORGE ADAMSON
Kora
15th. July 1971

Contents

Illustrations

Illustrations

All the above photographs were taken by Derek Cattani except for illustration 6, which is reproduced by permission of *Vanity Fair*.

A Lion
Called Christian

CHAPTER 1

A Lion with a Price Tag

No zoo is complete without lions. The small zoo at Ilfracombe on the Devon coast was no exception, and the lion and lioness were a particularly handsome pair. The lion had been bought from the Rotterdam Zoo, and the lioness from the Biblical Zoo in Jerusalem. They had their first litter on 12 August 1969; four healthy cubs, one male and three females. Nine weeks later, with summer over and no more holiday crowds to attract, two female cubs were sent to an animal dealer and were subsequently bought by a circus. The remaining female and the male were bought by Harrods, the Knightsbridge department store, and sent to London by train. The four cubs seemed destined, as their parents were, for a lifetime of frustration.

Three months before the cubs were born, we had left

1

Australia, uncertain of what lay ahead of us, but optimistic. We travelled independently for several months, but met up again in London, unexpectedly, in late November. Neither of us are conscientious sightseers, but one day in an unusual burst of enthusiasm we visited, amongst other tourist snares, the Tower of London. A suitable contrast, we decided, would be our first visit to Harrods. We were aware of Harrods' boast that they can provide anything, at a price of course. But they seemed to have extended themselves beyond our imagination, when on wandering into their zoo, we discovered two lion cubs in a small cage between the Siamese kittens and the old English sheep dogs. A lion cub with a price tag was not an easy thought to assimilate. The cubs were proving to be a successful drawcard for the Christmas shoppers, with the prospect of becoming the Christmas present for the person who already had everything.

We had not thought about lions before. Of course we had seen them at zoos, but this was as far as our interest and knowledge extended. Neither of us had even read *Born Free*. We sympathized with the cubs, for despite the efforts of the staff, they were incessantly disturbed by intrigued shoppers, yet we had to restrain the same urge within ourselves. Each person demanded a response.

The female snarled in an alarming manner and people were satisfied, but her brother pretended none of us existed. He was irresistible, and we sat, enchanted, beside their cage for hours.

"Why don't we buy him?"

"I've already named him Christian."

We intuitively knew that we were both serious, and a curious excitement began to grow. Even if it was only for a couple of months, surely we could offer him a better life than this? Or was it that we just wanted to take Christian away from everyone else, and have him to ourselves?

Suddenly our lives were to be incomplete without a lion cub. An impractical idea for two young Australians visiting Europe, but at least we could allow ourselves the luxury of investigating the possibility of buying him. We inquired if he was still for sale. The female had been sold, but the male was still available, for a modest two hundred and fifty guineas. A vast sum to us, but undaunted, we nonchalantly agreed that it seemed a very reasonable price. The assistant at the zoo suggested we speak to the buyer. He was, she pointedly warned us, interviewing any prospective purchasers very thoroughly, as it was important the lions did not fall into irresponsible hands.

We returned next morning looking more respectable, with our hair skilfully flattened, and wearing the tweed sportscoat our mothers, very perceptively, had insisted would be useful abroad, but up until now had been lying untouched at the bottom of our suitcases. We succeeded, with the help of a few tiny white lies, in convincing Mr. Roy Hazle, the buyer, that we would be responsible foster parents for a lion. Now, when Harrods was prepared to part with him, we had the first option to buy Christian.

Everything up until this point seemed very natural

and straightforward. We had gone shopping and had seen a lion that we liked, but could not take delivery for about three weeks. We lived in a small flat on the King's Road in Chelsea, above the shop where we were both about to begin work, and in all respects could not have been in a worse position to own any animal, least of all a lion. We spent days fruitlessly visiting estate agents, looking for a basement flat with a garden, "for our dog." It seemed pointless being truthful with them, when it was the landlords we really had to contend with. We were becoming very disheartened, but we decided to advertise in *The Times*, on the assumption that the courageous or eccentric landlord we had been unable to find, would probably be a reader of this newspaper.

> LION CUB, 2 young men seek suitable garden/roof, flat/house London. 352-7252.

The only response was a flood of telephone calls from other newspapers, prematurely wanting to photograph the lion.

In desperation, our last chance was to persuade the owners of the shop, Joe Harding and John Barnardiston, that in addition to us as employees, their business really needed a lion cub living on the premises. Particularly as the shop was called Sophisto-Cat. John was cautious by nature, being English, and fortunately was in Switzerland at the time. Joe was born in Kenya and had owned a variety of animals, and proved no opposition.

Christian could live in the basement of the shop, and it was to be a surprise for John. As we would be living above the shop, and working there, it seemed an ideal arrangement, for we could devote all the attention to Christian we realized would be necessary. Although it was an enormous basement, with several rooms, we also wanted to find a garden for him to exercise in.

We had friends living in a studio only three hundred yards from the shop, with access to a most suitable garden. Fully enclosed, and covering three quarters of an acre, it was owned by the Moravian Church. The minister, an ardent bird watcher, but not prejudiced against extending his zoological interests, very generously gave his permission for us to use the garden. As a result, we now felt able to assure Harrods that we could fulfil the practical requirements for owning a lion.

But while our excitement accelerated, we became rather frightened by our total ignorance of the sort of problems that faced us. We had no idea to what extent a lion could be domesticated, and were aware that we could be taking on an impossible and futile task. At Harrods we were told that the cubs had been handled by humans since birth, and that they both, particularly Christian, were responding to affection. He was the favourite, and appeared to have a delightful, even-tempered nature. As often as we could, we went to Harrods to play with the cubs when they were let out of their cage for an hour, after closing time. Naturally we wanted to spend as much time with him as possible, and it would make his transition to Sophisto-Cat and the King's Road easier if he was familiar with us. Both cubs were excessively playful, and while it was possible to handle them, they could be quite uncontrollable at times. They possessed extremely sharp teeth, and claws which they had not yet learnt to control, and it was difficult to avoid being scratched. Christian was definitely more accepting than his sister, and we assumed he would be less boisterous and hopefully more manageable when he was separated from her.

Mr. Hazle sensibly suggested that before we made our final decision, we talked to Charles Bewick and Peter Bowen, who had bought a puma from Harrods a year before. The puma, called Margot, was now fully grown, and although she seemed to have adjusted to life in London, it took some time for us to feel at ease with her. We were assured that she had an impeccable behaviour record, and because they had been able to devote considerable time to her, she was sufficiently domesticated to co-exist quite happily with them. It was encouraging, for they had obviously found the whole experience enjoyable, and much less complicated than they had anticipated. They looked forward to meeting Christian.

We realized it was unlikely that we would be able to have Christian for more than about six months. He would rapidly outgrow any environment we could create for him. We were determined to make these months as happy as we possibly could for Christian, but was it fair if he was then to go back to a zoo? Surely this would just make it harder for him, and the whole venture a marvellous indulgence for us. We decided to visit Longleat Lion Park, to see if it would be suitable for Christian. We were aware that when it had first opened, basic assumptions about lions had proved incorrect, and the lions had suffered casualties. Now, with the park extending over one hundred acres, and the lions divided into prides, they appeared to have created the best living conditions for lions in England. Mr. Roger Cawley, the manager, said he would be delighted to take Christian when he outgrew us.

Not only were we now in a position to have Christian, but we could also ensure that he would not spend the rest of his life in a zoo or in a circus. But still we both had very serious doubts. Were we really prepared to take on this enormous, binding responsibility? We could not ignore the fact that it was a lion, a basically wild animal and the most powerful predator after man, that we were bringing into our lives, and the lives of the people around us. We knew that a workable human-lion relationship was not an impossibility, but we could not be certain that we would attain this with Christian. He was now four months old and growing very quickly. Soon he would be capable of inflicting considerable damage. But while one of us talked of our recklessness and the risks, the other spoke of the novel and exciting experience that lay ahead. What finally united us was the staunch opposition, from most people we knew, to the idea of buying Christian. Unwittingly they intensified our determination to accept a challenge we might otherwise have resisted.

We collected Christian on 16 December 1969. Mr. Hazle waved good-bye, and with Christian sitting majestically and deceptively still on the back seat of the

7

car, we drove off towards the King's Road, extremely happy, but with an unvoiced suspicion and fear that we had committed ourselves to something that could prove just too big for us.

CHAPTER 2

Sophisto-Cat

It is a short drive from Harrods to Sophisto-Cat, but after months in a cage, Christian's world must have suddenly assumed the most enormous proportions. Frightened and confused, he scrambled all over us, and we had to stop frequently. We had no idea how we could even begin to control him. We tried to placate him with a huge Teddy bear that we had bought him as a welcoming present, but his total lack of interest in it left us helpless. Eventually we arrived at Sophisto-Cat, where friends impatiently waited. We carried him into the shop, and Christian, now much calmer, padded around investigating everything, and cleverly evaded all the hands that tentatively and incredulously reached down to pat him. He seemed only mildly disorientated, and he focused most of his attention on us, for presumably we represented the only link with his immediate past. We spent most of the night playing with him, Christian was ours.

A resident lion in the King's Road, Chelsea, was not too surprising. For a mile the road is scattered with trendy clothes shops, restaurants, clubs and antique markets. The façade is ephemeral, but the basic character remains the same; phoney, pretentious, but not without attraction. Every Saturday the road is blocked by a self-conscious parade of people and expensive cars. Tourists come to watch, while the others, in beautiful or freak clothes, came to be watched.

Sophisto-Cat sells antique pine furniture, and is situated in a curious area called the World's End, which marks the point where King Charles II's Road, and protection from highwaymen ended. A tradition that lingers on. A long way down the King's Road, the World's End is now part of fashionable Chelsea, and the locals resent the intrusion of a few smart antique and clothes shops.

Within two days Christian seemed to have fully adjusted to his new surroundings. Any initial inhibitions had vanished, and the Teddy bear was already in a million pieces. He enjoyed his greater freedom, and was much less boisterous without his sister. There was no indication that he missed her; perhaps we were some form of substitute, and, having none of the indifference common to most cats, he wanted to be near us. Now four months old, thirty pounds, and about two feet long, he was himself a larger-than-life Teddy bear. He loved being carried and cuddled, and his paws would gently reach around our necks and his tongue lick our faces. He had soft, tawny-coloured fur, and was surprisingly heavily spotted. Although well co-ordinated, his paws, head and ears were disproportionately large for the rest of his body, giving an indication of the size and strength of the animal he would grow into. But it was his beautiful, round, rust-coloured eyes that dominated his appearance. He had a delightful, placid nature, and he was so easy to manage that we felt that we had over-dramatized the problems of owning a lion. He was even house-trained. With the fastidiousness of all cats, he and his sister had used the same corner of their cage at Harrods, so we were optimistic. In one of the rooms in the basement we had installed a heater and put blankets for him to sleep on. In a corner we placed a lion-sized Kitty Litter tray. After two days of making indiscriminate puddles and messes, which we followed each time by a smack and then carrying him to the tray, this problem was solved. It all seemed too easy.

He was adaptable, and responsive to routine. His day began about 8 A.M. when one of us came downstairs from our flat to let him out. Although it seemed unnatural, quite often he had to be woken, and a sleepy, blinking little lion would affectionately greet us, and walk unsteadily over to squat on his tray. Then it was time to be fed. His first and last meals of the day were a mixture of Complan, Farex, and milk, with Abidec drops for additional vitamins. Sandy Lloyd, the assistant at Harrods Zoo, had adored the cubs and looked after them extremely well, and she provided us with a carefully balanced diet for Christian. Two main meals, given to him late in the morning and in the evening, consisted of three quarters of a pound of raw meat, a raw egg, and a spoonful of bone meal to prevent calcium deficiency. We varied the meat and occasionally gave him an unskinned rabbit. Christian always carried the skin around Sophisto-Cat for several days until it finally disintegrated. And he enjoyed having huge bones to play with and gnaw.

People's preconceptions about lions were often proved wrong in our experience; it is a fallacy that it is dangerous to give an animal such as a lion raw meat. We eyed rather enviously the delicious fillet steak that a French chef sometimes brought in for Christian. The chef loved lions and of course had access to plentiful supplies of meat. The quantity of meat Christian required increased weekly, and he became so expensive that we regretted not making him a vegetarian!

He was inexhaustibly playful. He had a variety of toys and rubber balls scattered all over the shop and the basement. Wastepaper baskets were a great favourite, first to be worn on the head, totally obscuring his sight, and then ripped apart. We had to buy him hardy toys, for the average life of a normal Teddy bear was about two minutes. He demanded our constant attention and it was impossible to ignore him. If one of us was reading a newspaper, or was on the telephone, Christian would immediately clamber on to his lap. Sophisto-Cat was a jungle of furniture, and he incessantly stalked us through it. He was an expert at creating games. He knew we would not allow him to jump on us, but he would cleverly manoeuvre himself into a position behind a piece of furniture, so that it appeared as if we were in fact temptingly hiding from him. Then with a clear conscience he would charge and leap on to us. We developed a habit of glancing nervously over our shoulders. If we noticed him frozen in a crouched position with intent, mischievous eyes, he would nonchalantly pretend to clean his paws, rather irritated that his fun had been spoiled, for the game was to stalk and catch us unawares. In a short time we could usually predict what his intentions were from the expression in his eyes. He was always entertaining, but very exhausting.

He looked forward each morning to the arrival of Kay Dew, the daily, for he was certain she had been provided for his enjoyment. He chased her brooms, rode on the vacuum cleaner, and stole or ate her dusters. She handled him very well, but warily watched the Farex and Complan smudges grow higher on the windows and glass doors.

When Christian first became part of the King's Road scene, he was small enough for us not to worry about letting him run around the shop with our customers. They rarely took seriously our initial warning, "Do you have any objection to lions?" One disbelieving woman, on seeing one of Christian's bones said, "That bone is at least lion-sized." "That's what we tried to tell you, look behind you." She watched incredulously as Christian ambled past to claim his bone. Usually it was good for business. Even the English had to react to a lion cub stretched out on the pine table they were contemplating buying. Most people were delighted, and no one complained about the occasional laddered stocking.

Many women returned with sceptical husbands and friends, and carloads of children on Saturdays. Saturdays, with the familiar King's Road parade were busy anyway, and Sophisto-Cat suddenly acquired a zoo or circus atmosphere. To dispel this, Christian had to spend most of the day in the basement, and only the particularly disappointed, or the particularly attractive, could persuade us to take them downstairs to see him.

Every afternoon he went to his garden for exercise. Harrods had given us a collar and leash for him. The collar looked incongruous, but it was necessary as it made it easier to hold him, and he quickly forgot about it. At first we tried to walk him to the garden on his leash, as it was only three hundred yards. But he never walked, just sprinted for a few yards and then resolutely sat down. He was frightened of the traffic, and people crowded round him. We dreaded meeting other animals, for although he did not appear very interested in them, they were a welcome diversion. For the first few weeks we could just pick him up and carry him, but he soon grew much heavier, and the short walk became an ordeal. While it would have been easier if he had walked on a leash, it was unfair to expect such unnatural behaviour from a lion, so we did not persist, and resorted to driving him there in the car, or in the Sophisto-Cat van. He was always manageable in both, but restless, as lions can never fully accept any form of restriction.

The garden was ideal. No humans, no animals, and it was surrounded by a high brick wall. This wall dates from the Tudor period, and the present studios and the old Moravian chapel in the garden are built on the foundations of Sir Thomas More's stables. After a succession of eminent owners, Sir Hans Sloane sold the property in 1750 to Count Zinzendorf of Saxony, who bought the land to found a Moravian settlement in England. The Moravians were among the first independent Protestants and had formed their brotherhood in 1457 when they protested against the moral corruption and political activity of the Roman Catholic Church in Bohemia. They take the name Moravians, rather than Bohemians, from the group of refugees from Moravia who settled on Count Zinzendorf's estate in Saxony in 1722. The count's son, Christian Renatus, Count of Zinzendorf and Pottendorf, is buried in the garden. Actually it is a graveyard. The Moravians, most fortunately, bury their dead very neatly and unostentatiously, so this was not at all obvious.

There was a large area of grass for Christian to play on, and trees and hedges to hide behind. Interestingly, it took several weeks for him to adjust to all the space, and he would not go out into the centre of the garden, away from the protection of the hedges. But then the garden became his established territory, and he adored it. He loved chasing and jumping on to us, but we thought this was an inadvisable habit to encourage in a lion, so we kicked footballs for him to chase instead. He was remarkably fast, and beautifully co-ordinated. He would run after the ball, pounce on it, and dramatically roll over and over with it. The few times it snowed, he loved skidding through it, and was not worried by the cold. If he ever had us in an awkward position on the ground when we were playing, he seemed to sense his

15

advantage and get a surge of new energy which alarmed us, and appeared to mystify him. We spent about an hour a day at the garden, which seemed adequate, for he was rarely reluctant to return to Sophisto-Cat. Besides, it was time for his favourite occupation.

Late in the afternoons Christian would sit regally on the furniture in the shop window, heavily spotlighted, and watch the activities of the World's End. He was the star attraction, and the people there loved him and were immensely proud of him. He seemed to belong to all of them. In the window he drew appreciative crowds of regular admirers or astonished newcomers. These were happy hours. If there were too many people and his view was obscured, he simply changed windows. Several motorists, seeing Christian unself-consciously displaying himself, bumped into the cars in front. And a conversation was overheard between a child and his mother on a passing bus: "Mummy, there was a lion in that shop window!" "Don't be ridiculous. If you don't stop this lying, I'll get your father to thrash you."

CHAPTER 3

Noblesse Oblige

We had not told Christian that he was a lion. We thought this knowledge would only lead to regrettable lion-like behaviour. We avoided using the word "lion" in front of him, but occasionally had to spell out L-I-O-N to ignorant people, who thought Christian was a leopard because of his spots. He enjoyed looking at himself in the large mirrors at Sophisto-Cat, so while he must have been confused as to what sort of animal he was, he knew exactly what he looked like. He often accompanied us in the car, and as there are more sculptured lions in London than there are live ones in Africa, we decided to tell him the truth, before he discovered it himself and asked awkward questions. We drove him to Trafalgar Square to see the lions at the base of Nelson's Column. He recognized himself imme-

diately, and was delighted to be such an obvious symbol
of nobility. Fortunately this information did not alter
his behaviour, for he had, after all, assumed superiority
over us from the beginning. But too much knowledge
could be dangerous, so we asked the Moravian minister
not to tell Christian that the early Christians had been
fed to the lions.

Consistent with their standards, Harrods had sold us a
lion of quality. He was very healthy and had a beautiful
nature. He was even-tempered, and not easily alarmed or
frightened. These qualities were reinforced by his trust
in us and his strong feeling of security. The fact that
his behaviour was predictable and consistent made living
with him much easier than it could have been. We felt
our way very carefully with him, and learnt about him
quickly. We rarely misjudged his intentions.

It was easy to recognize a psychological organization
in him which could be expressed in human terms. To us,
his personality resembled a human personality. His
"sense of humour" seemed very similar to ours. If he
tripped over something, and he tended to be rather
clumsy for a lion, he appeared embarrassed but would
quickly pretend as most people do, that nothing had
happened. Lions can communicate with humans much
more closely than almost all other animals. It has taken
a very long time for the two most powerful predators in
the world to discover that they have so much in common.

Christian's personality was immense, and his presence
entirely filled the shop and our lives. We realized that if
the months he was to live with us were to be as happy
for him as we intended, he had to be allowed as much

natural expression as possible. For him to remain the unfrustrated, even-tempered animal he was, it was necessary, in addition to giving him all the time and affection we had, to minimize any restriction.

We attained a relationship of mutual respect, with no hint from him of domestic-animal subservience. We made no attempt to dominate him, and in our experience this would probably have had disastrous consequences. Besides, it is doubtful if a lion can ever be totally dominated, perhaps just precariously controlled. And a lion's respect is not easily earned. Christian had a determined character, but he seemed to realize that he had to co-operate, and he quickly knew what sort of behaviour would not be allowed.

He hated being ignored, and was very conscious of the effect he had on people. He could not resist testing the reactions of newcomers, and always remembered if people had not coped well with him previously. If customers had not noticed him sitting on the stairs in the shop, he would grunt to attract their attention. From this commanding position, his paws knocked off several hats and pairs of glasses. He was extremely curious, and his eyes were always watching, searching for anything new that had to be investigated.

It was his eyes that were his most arresting feature. They were expressive, intelligent eyes that could concentrate on us with love and trust, or challenge us, but sometimes stare straight through us, beyond to a region from which we were excluded.

Christian possessed a memory for people and places, and in human terms showed a degree of intelligence.

He quickly learnt how to open the door of the room in which he slept, if it was not locked. He kept his food for the day on the top of various cupboards in the office at the back of the shop. He cleverly managed to climb high enough on other furniture, in order to stand up on his hind legs, and knock his food to the floor.

Lions are gregarious animals. Christian constantly entertained us, and he knew we were a devoted audience. He regarded us as his family, and was tremendously affectionate towards us. Lions greet each other with a rather ceremonial touching of heads, and we always knelt to enable him to do this with us. Any parting from him, regardless of its duration, involved another fond greeting, a lick and a cuddle. He enjoyed being close, often either leaning against us, or actually sitting on us. Sometimes he would dramatically leap from the ground into our arms. Of course he could be arrogant and demanding, but if he had to be disciplined, either verbally or with a smack, he accepted it, and did not bear any resentment. He was very much aware if we were displeased with him, and if he felt it was deserved, he would make obvious, and always successful attempts to win us over again.

Christian was particularly unaggressive and unpossessive about his food, which indicated that in some respects he was an exceptional lion. He had no other animals to compete with, and this and the knowledge that he was fed regularly must have been contributing factors. But people who knew a great deal more about lions than we did were always astounded by his attitude towards his food. He had a healthy appetite, and in his eagerness he often knocked his food out of our hands before we had time to place it on the floor for him. But we could take his food away from him if it was necessary, even out of his mouth. He loved the marrow inside bones, but as he was unable to get it out, he gently ate it from the tips of our fingers.

Lions depend to a large extent on their mouths for communication and contact. He licked us to show his affection. His rough tongue always tested surfaces for their taste and texture. He had sharp milk teeth, and while he enjoyed mouthing our hands and arms, he quickly learnt not to bite us. There were moods, however, in which his mouth just hung open, waiting to be filled. Kneecaps were a suitable height. Our clothes were often damaged by his teeth or claws getting caught, and we sometimes resorted to wearing extremely unattractive bottle-green boiler suits.

A lion needs to exercise his claws and jaws on wood. In the first few weeks, several table and chair legs were damaged. However, after a few smacks he gave this up, especially when he realized he could use the banisters on the stairs in the shop, or in the basement, instead. And lions are creatures of habit. They are earth-bound in comparison with other cats, and he did not jump all over the furniture. But he enjoyed surveying his domain from a height, and would often sit on tables and chests of drawers. Fortunately, he preferred the stairs which gave him greater height, and he would sit with a paw dangling elegantly over the side. Actually he damaged very little furniture, and this only occurred if he slipped and dug his claws in for support. Rather unwisely, a very expensive table had been superbly set with cutlery, china, glasses and candles, in the middle of the shop. We heard the sound of breaking glass, and immediately knew what had happened. In the confusion Christian moved his weight to one side of the table, and he and the table-top crashed to the floor. The table had been sold, and now there were several deep scratches on it. We telephoned the woman who had bought it to apologize. "Don't worry," she said, "I only came into the shop to see Christian, the table was an afterthought. Please don't worry about the scratches, they will remind me of that beautiful lion." But he could never resist attacking the mattress on a brass bed in the shop. This problem was only solved when a friend very generously brought Christian a mattress of his own, and, wildly excited, Christian dragged it down to the basement, although it was much bigger and heavier than he was.

His formidably sharp claws were initially a major concern. Before he learnt to control them we received many scratches. But within two months he developed more control over them, and he also realized that we stopped playing with him if we were scratched. He learnt to keep them sheathed, but if he was wrestling with something such as his mattress, pretending it was a zebra he had just stalked and thrown to the ground, we had to remember that his claws would instinctively be out.

Christian, like all lions, was fascinated by children. We were always extremely careful, and held him if children were in the shop. One day a photographer from a local newspaper was taking a photograph of him, on a leash, outside Sophisto-Cat. A woman, probably thinking

Christian was a dog, strode in front of him with her two-year-old child, also on a leash. Christian curiously extended one paw, and knocked the child to the pavement. One of us grabbed Christian while the other obscured the photographer from the sort of photograph the newspapers crave for. The child was slightly dazed, but so swaddled with clothes it could not have been hurt. At first the mother was furious, but as she returned later with endless friends, and other children to dangle in front of him, she was apparently delighted with the incident.

But he grew very quickly. Within two months the beginnings of a mane developed and he suddenly looked quite adult. It was unfair, and probably unwise, to expect innocent customers to cope with a lion springing from behind a chest of drawers, and clasping them around their thighs with his huge paws. He left most people alone, but like many other animals, he instinctively knew those who were frightened, and he enjoyed teasing them. Obviously we could not risk any incidents, and no insurance company was prepared to cover us in the event of one.

We began to feel the weight of the responsibility of owning Christian. He had to spend much more time in the basement, and was only permitted in the shop when there were no customers. He enjoyed being in the basement, and he had many toys to play with, but he resented not having the freedom to go up to the shop when he wished. Sometimes he would unnecessarily squat on his Kitty Litter tray, as an unsubtle sign that he was ready to go upstairs. Lions are happy to sleep if there is nothing better to do, but his hours in the basement were broken by many visits. The others at Sophisto-Cat, Joe and John the owners, and particularly Jenny Taylor the manageress, adored Christian, and he was just as fond of them. Usually at least one of us would be downstairs playing with him. When people came to see him we took them down, and in the basement it was easier for us to be in complete control of the situation, and if necessary prevent him from jumping on them. He was an unusually accepting lion and there were very few people he disliked. It was difficult to discover what he objected to; sometimes it may have been a strong perfume or an after-shave lotion, and he always jumped up on one friend of ours, but only when he wore a particular coat.

We tried to keep him unaware of just how much, or how little control we had over him. After the first few months it took him a surprisingly long time to realize that although we could still carry him, if he struggled we had to release him immediately. If he played too roughly with us, we stopped, and because of this, he never knew the point where he had in fact become stronger than we were. For a lion he was very obedient, and he usually co-operated with us. Only rarely would he ignore our smacks, and when this happened, there was very little we could do. We just had to pretend that we were not worried by what he was doing, rather than let him know that we could not stop him.

Lions give extremely clear and fair warnings of their displeasure. With their strength, teeth, and claws, it would be foolish to disregard them. Only once in the months that Christian lived at Sophisto-Cat, were we exceedingly frightened of him. He found a fur belt that had dropped off a coat, and delighted by his find, he ran down into the basement. We followed him to retrieve it. He was chewing the belt and making excited sucking sounds. We knew that this would be something he would be reluctant to give up. We tried to take it from him, but he flattened his ears and snarled a ferocious warning. He was an unrecognizable, wild animal. Undoubtedly he would have attacked us if we had tried again to take the belt from him. We wanted to leave him, but slowly moved a few yards away, and talked to one another as if nothing had happened, and as if we had forgotten about the belt. We realized we must not convey to him how frightened we were. It could have encouraged him to repeat this performance if he had sensed how effective it was. After about five minutes his excitement over the belt, and his anger, subsided. We spent the next few hours talking and playing with him very normally. We respected him for his distinct warning. This incident was never repeated, but we had been given an important reminder of Christian's potential dangerousness.

CHAPTER 4

"The Publicity-shy Jungle King"

The most embarrassing situation that occurred while Christian lived at Sophisto-Cat, was when the Lady Mayor of Chelsea came into the shop to meet him. She bent over to stroke him and her elaborate chain of office dangled temptingly in front of him. He could not resist, and a large paw went out and swiped at it. The chain whirled around her neck. She was dazed but unhurt. Lions, monarchs by birth, are not impressed by the trappings of municipal offices.

An interesting assortment of people met Christian, and some of them visited him regularly. There was a woman who came into the shop with jelly-babies for the bear she heard lived there. She was greatly disappointed to hear that Christian was only a lion, and worse, was not tempted by the jelly-babies. Diana Rigg and Mia Farrow, customers at Sophisto-Cat, were his two favourite actresses. As Christian received considerable publicity, several people came into the shop concerned that we were just using him as a gimmick. All of them seemed placated to see him so happy, healthy, and apparently very fond of us.

Having a lion became part of our lives and we had to accept all the interest he aroused. If we were not with him we were expected to talk about him. We had to listen patiently to people's stories about their "wild" cats, while others reminisced of their experiences in Africa. But their stories and questions seemed to have very little relevance to Christian, living so ludicrously out of context in London. We were constantly asked, "How long is it before he becomes a man-eater?" It was impossible to relate such questions to Christian, especially when watching him play with his best friend, Unity Bevis.

Unity met Christian in January 1970, one month after we had bought him. She heard that a lion lived at Sophisto-Cat, and rushed immediately to the shop. She visited Christian every afternoon, and her life revolved around him. She was so slight we were worried that he would unintentionally hurt her, but she learnt to handle him extremely well. She wore a thick coat and a rather mad felt hat for protection. This hat obscured most of her face, and it was only when Christian finally ate the hat several weeks later that we realized how attractive she was.

Unity was addicted to lions. One day in Rome she had decided that she wanted a lion, although she had not known any before. She managed to persuade the Rome Zoo to sell her a nine-month-old lioness who had just arrived at the zoo from Africa, and had never been handled by humans before. It did not occur to Unity to be frightened of lions, and she was surprised when her flatmate locked herself in her bedroom for a fortnight, after Lola the lioness was delivered in a crate. Unity found landlords just as unreasonable, and estimates that in the year and a half she and Lola lived together they moved about twenty times. Unity had to return to England, and Lola now lives with friends near Naples. Unity had an extraordinary affinity with Christian, and we could understand how she had managed to have a successful and accident-free relationship with Lola, under much more difficult circumstances.

Each afternoon when Unity arrived at Sophisto-Cat, Christian could be heard in the basement, noisily playing football with something, usually a plastic bucket. At the sound of her footsteps on the stairs, he would stop playing and listen and wait to see who it was. Unity would say: "Hello, Christian, it's me." Christian would grunt loudly, his normal greeting, and jump up at the locked door, to peer at her through a small round hole. To prevent him from running upstairs when she opened the door, Unity would ask Christian to move away, before she came in. Although still close to the door, with a lion-like miaow he would indicate that it was safe for her to come in. "No," she would say, "that's not far enough, go farther away." After a brief silence, Christian would grunt, and if the grunt sounded sufficiently distant to Unity's experienced ears, she then went into the basement and shut the door behind her. Christian would rush to greet her fondly and, grabbing her by the coat, would enthusiastically lead her around the basement.

If he was too boisterous, and pretended not to hear when she said, "Don't be too rough," or "Stop it, Christian," she would edge towards the door when he was not looking, and leave him. Christian would run to the door and miaow and grunt. We would hear Unity say, "You're very naughty, and if you don't behave, I'm not coming in to play with you. I'm not a bucket, and I don't expect to be treated like one." As an apology, a few sorrowful grunts would follow, getting farther and farther from the door, to show Unity she could come in without his rushing upstairs. Reprimanded, but always forgiven, he would now be gentle with her, and they would entertain each other with games and conversation for the rest of the afternoon.

One of Christian's most endearing characteristics was that he had individual relationships with all of us; only subtle differences, but different greetings, different games and tricks, and he knew exactly what each of us would let him get away with. Unity could never bring herself to refuse him anything. She often came to the garden with us, and the hours she spent with him each day in the basement made an enormous contribution to keeping him gentle and unfrustrated. Animals have personalities that people rarely give them a chance to express or develop, and Unity taught us just how diverse Christian's was.

We gave more time and affection to Christian than

1. "... and there were no casualties ..."

2.   Christian with the authors on King's Road

3. His favourite position on the stairs in Sophisto-Cat

4. In the shop

5. The flat above Sophisto-Cat

6. Our faces are our fortunes.

8. Football in the Moravian Close

9. "Christian, like all lions, was fascinated by children."

10.   In the Moravian Close

11.   Christian between the coats of arms of Lords Burleigh
      and Lincoln, former owners of the garden

12. A & B   Christian meets Bill Travers and Jack de Manio.

13.   Christian's caravan at Leith Hill

14. Christian gets a little too boisterous at Leith Hill.

either of us had consciously given to anything or any-body else before, and it gave our lives a sense of purpose we had not previously felt. Our days were spent with him, and at nights we put him in his room in the basement, if we wanted to go out. One of us, quite often both of us at different hours, would let him out for a run around the shop late at night, before going to bed. As the shop was closed on Sundays, and Christian enjoyed any change of environment, we sometimes took him on outings. But there are not many places you can take a lion in London. One day we took him to Kensing-ton Gardens. He was frightened by all the space, and although on a long leash, he just hugged the fence for security. Not surprisingly, so many people gathered around him that it made this and similar outings to parks impossible.

We telephoned a Dr. Barnardo's Home to see if the children would enjoy a visit from Christian. The woman we spoke to was rather surprised, but when we assured her that he was not "dangerous," she accepted. We told her it was inadvisable for Christian to be actually with the children, and we asked if there was an enclosed area for him. She suggested that the children could safely watch from inside the building, while "the lion grazes on the grass outside"!

But Christian's visit met with an unexpected lack of interest. Little faces were pressed against the windows for a few minutes, then the children returned to their toys. While we had afternoon tea with the children, Christian was shut in a room. But a mischievous child let him out, and he came to look for us. The children

31

screamed, scattered, and scrambled on to chairs and tables. Leaving chaos and probably many nightmares behind, we drove a confused little lion back to Sophisto-Cat.

Owning a lion increased the quantity, if not necessarily the quality of our acquaintances in London. Christian was often invited to visit people, and he did visit several friends, but only once each. The one household geared to incorporating a visit from a lion was that shared by Charles Bewick, Peter Bowen, and Margot the puma. We visited them quite often, and Christian spent Christmas Day there, while we went to friends in the country. Christian had been specifically not invited. Margot was a beautiful animal with an attractive purr, but her behaviour was unpredictable, and it was difficult to relax in her company. We had hoped, rather naïvely, that Margot and Christian would be friends as we did not know any dogs strong enough to be his playmates. But Margot was a different species, a different sex, and a year older, and she was intensely antagonistic towards him. He was just indifferent. In fairness to her, Christian was an intruder on her territory. It was possible to have them in the same room together, but the only time he approached her, Margot whipped her paw at him and scratched his velvety nose. Christian did not care, but we were furious because he was to appear on television the next day.

In the middle of January 1970, a month after we had bought him, Thames Television heard that a lion was living at Sophisto-Cat, and asked us about Christian appearing on "Magpie," their children's magazine programme. He was only to appear for a few minutes so we thought we could cope with it. We drove out to the television studios at Teddington, rather excited but uncertain as to how Christian would behave. Unfortunately we had to have several rehearsals before the live performance, and we felt this was rather unnecessary, as Christian reacted differently each time, and was increasingly less co-operative. He was confused and dazzled by the glaring studio lights, and frightened by the cameras which advanced on him. He was irritated at having to spend so much time on a leash, but long-suffering rather than angry. We regretted having accepted "Magpie's" invitation, and nervously waited for the live performance. It was impossible to predict what Christian would do. One of us was to be interviewed, and at the same time try and keep Christian in camera range. He was apparently a great success, although what appeared to be a playful romp on the studio floor, was in reality a struggle to stop him from running away.

Before his appearance on television, only a few newspapers had been interested in Christian. But suddenly there was much more curiosity, although the people who interviewed us seemed disappointed that owning a lion was less complicated than they expected. The photographs they published were always of Christian yawning, with his teeth bared, and of course they appeared as vicious snarls. The publicity was good for Sophisto-Cat, but we realized that if it was to continue we had to have control over the photographs published, so that Christian could at least be portrayed accurately. We found a photographer who got on well with him, and a pictorial record of his life in London began. The newspapers were quite welcome to buy a photograph if they wanted one.

People often came into the shop wanting to use Christian in television commercials, or for various promotional purposes. He was such an expense for us that we were prepared to be mildly commercial, on condition that he suffered no unhappiness because of it. He did a "Nights on the Wild Side" series for a fashion magazine, advertising nightgowns. It was easy work, for he was just required to lie on a bed with a beautiful model, and be photographed. The caption read:

Beware the man-hunting feline! Some stalk their prey in the jungle; others play pussy at home in lounging lingerie that clings and ripples with the same cat-like grace. Our lingerie isn't meant for lonesome evenings—put it on when you're planning to pounce, and if he doesn't, then get another cat for company!

Christian always enjoyed chewing hair, and the model had masses of it. He planned to pounce, and she became rather frightened, and was actually heard to say: "My face is my fortune!" Restrained, Christian bit a hole in the goatskin bedspread and destroyed two satin pillows instead.

Several months later BOAC contacted us. They were opening a new route to Africa, and wanted Christian to make a very brief appearance at a promotional function. He created quite a sensation and easily outshone the other African representatives; potted palm trees and avocadoes. He earned thirty guineas, which we paid into his account at the bank. We had photographs taken of Christian opening this account for their house journal. It was an easy way of pacifying the manager about our overdrafts. We also did a series of Easter photographs for the newspapers, of Christian with six little chickens. Christian was amazingly gentle and there were no casualties.

When he was about seven months old, and obviously leaving his cub days behind, there was suddenly a much greater and more widespread public interest. People were astounded that he was still so easy to manage. We were interviewed by several American and Australian newspaper and broadcasting services and Jack de Manio, of the early morning "Today" programme on BBC radio telephoned to invite Christian to be interviewed. At our suggestion he came into Sophisto-Cat to meet Christian beforehand, and we warned him that Christian could be very inarticulate if he was not in the mood. A disadvantage in a radio interview. As Christian had not yet roared, it was unlikely that Mr. de Manio's would be treated to his first attempt.

A car was sent to Sophisto-Cat at 6:30 A.M. the next morning, and the three of us were taken to Broadcasting House. When we arrived the commissionaire blocked our entry to the building and, scarcely glancing at what was on the end of the leash, he challenged:

"No dogs allowed in here—it's the regulations."

"Do your regulations extend to lions?" we asked.

But people do not argue with lions, and as we strode past him into the building, he nimbly jumped aside.

The programme began, but Christian was far too interested in investigating the paraphernalia in the radio studio, and looking at the faces pressed against the windows, even to consider making any lion-like noises. We spoke briefly on his behalf. He was, however, most offended by the caption in the next day's *Daily Mail*:

Mike-shy Christian flops on radio.

We were mystified when we received a telephone call from the BBC at Sophisto-Cat later in the day. Without being offered any explanation, we were curtly asked Christian's value. It was not a question we had had reason to consider, but we told them what he had cost us. Several days later we read in Charles Greville's column in the *Daily Mail* what had happened. The caption was:

The Lion Behind Bars of Red Tape.

BBC regulations stated that animals brought into the building had to be insured, but because of some slip-up, "an hilarious situation built up with poker-faced officialdom going about the business of taking out a policy against damage to their departed guests. And, presumably, damage to the hosts, although as events had already shown by that time, the animal could hardly raise a yawn in the studio, let alone breakfast off de Manio and his team . . . and the value of the publicity-shy jungle king? £500 say the owners."

Newspapers invariably rang us if anywhere in the world a lion, or other big cat, had attacked or damaged someone. We enjoyed disappointing them with glowing reports of Christian's impeccable behaviour. Good news is no news. So many papers were inaccurate in their information about Christian, that it was surprising we only received one hostile letter. After an article had appeared in an American newspaper in April 1970, a woman wrote a long abusive letter. She concluded: "What do you intend doing with him when you tire of him? He must now be growing up and after the life you have forced him to lead, he must be getting vicious and dangerous. No doubt you have had his claws and perhaps even his teeth removed, so I'm sure no zoo would want him. End his miserable life and have him put to sleep." Incorrect as she was about Christian's life with us at Sophisto-Cat, we shared her concern for his future.

CHAPTER 5

A Proposal

By April 1970, Christian was bored. He was now eight months old and rapidly outgrowing Sophisto-Cat. Life had become repetitive and seemed to contain very few surprises for him. He was irritated that he had outgrown his favourite sitting spot on the stairs. It was too easy for him to climb all over the furniture in the shop, and now weighing 130 pounds, he was heavy enough to break the plate-glass windows accidentally. He required more freedom, while we could only give him less. If he chose to behave badly and he was now capable of inflicting serious damage we feared we could not control him. Whereas he had previously been an attraction, his size was beginning to frighten customers away. George Lazenby, of James Bond fame, came to the shop with a friend of ours one afternoon. Christian was sitting in the window and even George could not be persuaded to enter the shop. So Christian was spending most of his time in the basement, and increasingly resented any form of restriction.

He was less contented and so we were we. It became an enormous strain on us. We had a responsibility towards Christian, but also the responsibility for not creating a situation that could be dangerous. It was inadvisable to wait and see what outlet his frustrations might take.

The question of his future, which had hung over us from the very beginning, now inescapably confronted us. We went to Longleat Lion Park again, for as we had discovered before we bought Christian, they seemed to offer the best living conditions for lions in England. This time we knew more about lions. Because of the likelihood that Christian would soon be going there, we were proudly, but mistakenly, shown other sides of Longleat. We saw what an enormous commercial concern the Longleat–Chipperfield partnership was, for apart from the lions in the Park, Mary Chipperfield provides an animal-hiring service for film and television companies. Also, some of the lions that we saw were apparently part of a travelling circus. It was doubtful if we could ensure that Christian would be introduced into a pride and live in the Park, and not used for more obvious commercial purposes. For Christian, Longleat was not a satisfactory solution.

To send him to a zoo would have been a betrayal of faith difficult for us, but much more difficult for him, to live with. We hoped to find someone with a large country estate who could take him, and feel about him the same way that we did. To look for another alternative we visited several private zoos. They were perhaps more rural than their city counterparts, but more amateur, and as restricting and insensitive.

One afternoon Bill Travers and his wife, Virginia McKenna, came into the shop. As they had starred in the film *Born Free*, the story of Elsa, the lioness who had been returned to the wild by Joy and George Adamson, we thought that their association with lions had brought them to Sophisto-Cat. Disappointingly, they were only shopping for a pine desk but we were unable to resist the opportunity, and nonchalantly saying that we had a surprise for them, we asked them to follow us downstairs. They were astonished to see a lion run towards us and greet us affectionately. We talked about Christian's life with us, and they understood our dilemma about his future. Bill and Virginia had a much greater knowledge of lions than we had, and we asked them endless questions. We were flattered when they said they would like to come and see Christian again.

A few days later Bill came into Sophisto-Cat with James Hill, who was introduced to us as the director of the film *Born Free*. We wondered why James had come, and why he questioned us so extensively about Christian. We were surprised and delighted when Bill invited us to dinner at his house at Leith Hill in Surrey. He said he would like to show us a documentary film he had made about lions that had begun their lives in captivity.

Dinner with film stars. It seemed fitting that James

Hill should collect us from Sophisto-Cat in his Rolls-Royce, and to the astonishment of the World's Enders, we were grandly swept down to Surrey. After dinner we watched Bill's film *The Lions Are Free*, showing what had since happened to the lions involved in the filming of *Born Free*. Twenty-four lions had been used, yet, contrary to the theme of the film, only after a long struggle by Joy, George, Bill, and Virginia, was George allowed to rehabilitate three of them. None of the others would have the chance to live a natural life. In *The Lions Are Free* Bill visited the three lions George had successfully rehabilitated, and although they had not seen him for three years they remembered him, and he received a fond greeting.

The film ended with Virginia visiting Whipsnade Zoo, to see Little Elsa, a lioness she had become particularly fond of during the filming of *Born Free*. Virginia called, and Little Elsa immediately recognized her, and ran to the bars of the compound. How could Virginia explain why they could not greet each other as they always had, or justify Little Elsa's miserable life? The parallel with Christian was only too apparent, with the probability that within weeks we would have to condemn him to the same meaningless existence. Sensing our feelings, Bill smiled and said: "I think we can help you solve the problem of Christian's future. We would like to arrange for him to be flown out to Africa where George Adamson can rehabilitate him into the life for which he was intended."

It was as if a death-sentence had suddenly, simply, been lifted. Of all the lions ever born in Europe,

Christian had been given an unprecedented reprieve. He was to go back to where he belonged. Bill had telephoned George Adamson in Kenya after his initial introduction to Christian at Sophisto-Cat. George was extremely interested in the experiment of bringing a lion from England for rehabilitation in Africa, and was confident that it would be successful. Bill and James intended making a television film in order to cover the considerable expense involved.

There was no question of our having to be converted to Bill and Virginia's proposal. But our immediate reaction was that Christian had led such an unnatural life, we were worried we might have de-lionized him to an extent that made rehabilitation impossible. George had assured Bill that Christian was still very young, and that it would take many more centuries of lions existing in captivity before their natural instincts would be impaired. George intended to creat a man-made pride of lions, incorporating Christian. Bill wanted us to accompany Christian to Kenya, and help him start to adjust to his new life. George would live with the lions and feed them until they had established their territory, and were functioning effectively as a pride.

We realized it could not be assumed that Christian would have a long, natural life. Lions have to face territorial battles with one another, or droughts and scarcity of game which only the strongest survive. Also the youngest in the pride eats last. When lions hunt animals as large as buffaloes, unless they kill efficiently, they can easily be injured, or killed themselves. And Christian, with his Chelsea background, would be starting with disadvantages. However he would escape a long, safe but totally pointless life in captivity, and would be given the opportunity to take his chance in his natural environment.

On our way back to London we spoke excitedly of the unpredictability of life. Where would Christian be now if someone else had bought him at Harrods? What would have happened if Bill and Virginia had not come into Sophisto-Cat? By accident, they walked into our problem of Christian's future, and became involved in it. By buying Christian we had added new dimensions to our lives, and now unexpectedly, to his. It would have been an unforgettable experience, but totally spoiled by the fate that had seemed inevitable. Bill and Virginia now offered the perfect ending to our relationship with Christian.

CHAPTER 6

The Lion at World's End

Bill flew to Kenya to assist in negotiations which had
already begun with the Kenyan Government. He was
confident that this unusual project would be acceptable,
but the plans became more complicated than had been
anticipated. In principle, permission to make the documentary was not a problem. It would be good publicity
for Kenya and attract more tourists. Tourism is the
main industry, and even if the basic motivation is to
maintain this industry, there is an increasing awareness
among most African governments of the need for the
conservation and protection of animals. The Kenyan
Government was also interested in having a record of
George Adamson's methods of rehabilitating lions, and
particularly the scientific documentation of such an experiment with a London lion.

However, there had been considerable controversy in Kenya the previous year over the whole question of the rehabilitation of lions. A child had been injured by one of George Adamson's lions, and this unfortunate incident provided an unfavourable background to our negotiations. Some members of the government viewed the rehabilitation of lions as a worthwhile project, but others felt that because of their earlier contact with humans, these lions would be likely to approach people in the Game Parks, and that dangerous situations could arise. Most people fear lions, and for Africans, they are a traditional natural enemy, so why bring yet another potential man-eater from England?

But the Kenyan Government decided to give their permission for Christian to come to Kenya, if a suitable area could be found. It had to have water and game, and be in a region where there were no tourists, nor any likelihood of a tourist area developing. It would have to be closed to hunting, and have no resident Africans or their cattle as an easy temptation for the lions. Bill looked at several possibilities while he was in Kenya, but had to return to England, leaving George to continue the search.

Meanwhile we had not heard from Bill and Virginia for several weeks. We did not dare telephone them in case we were told that it was no longer possible for Christian to go to Kenya. Finally Bill rang and explained the delay, and he told us that George had just found two suitable areas, and it seemed likely that the Kenyan Government would agree to the use of either.

Bill was confident enough to decide that filming would

begin at Sophisto-Cat the following Monday. The film, to be called *The Lion at World's End*, would be directed by James Hill, and was to start with a reconstruction of Bill and Virginia's meeting with Christian, and then record the story exactly as it happened. Through the influential medium of television, this film would help to attract attention to the desperate need for the protection and conservation of animals. And Christian, through extraordinary luck, was to be the subject and prime beneficiary of the film.

Our excitement was mixed with apprehension. After our experience at the television studios when Christian had appeared on the children's programme, we realized that it was impossible to predict how he would react to being filmed. We did not know to what extent we would be involved, although, having no ambitions in this field, we could reject the old theatrical axiom "Never compete with animals or children."

Bill and James gave strict instructions that Sophisto-Cat was to remain unchanged for the filming. But as it would be closed to customers for one or two days, we thought it would be a nice gesture to the owners, Joe and John, if the shop appeared as smart as possible. On Sunday we repainted the walls and floor. It was a nicer gesture than we had intended, for it was an enormous shop and we worked hard all day. Christian was only allowed upstairs late in the afternoon, after the paint had dried on the floor. The last wall was still being completed, and Christian knocked over the tin, splashing paint everywhere. Surprised, he jumped back, but slipped and fell. Scrambling to his paws, he then ran to the other end of the shop. We were appalled; white paw marks covered the black floor. And Christian, required to appear as a lion for the cameras next morning, was an unrecognizable white animal. Until very late that night one of us was repainting the floor, while in the basement, the other, armed with towels and turps, was struggling to clean Christian, who just thought it was a new game.

Next day Sophisto-Cat was transformed into a film set. At first Christian was dazzled by the bright lights and confused by all the unfamiliar equipment and camera crew. But this helped to keep him unusually subdued, and he only scattered the crew a few times. Bill and James are familiar with filming animals, and were very patient and undemanding. Christian, bored with the normal shop routine, enoyed the day, and was so co-operative that Bill described him as a "one-take lion." We were to participate fully in the film and we could forget about the cameras by concentrating, rather intensely, on Christian, who performed magnificently.

The following day we filmed at the Moravian Close, but Christian resented sharing his garden with so many other people and was very unco-operative. This was probably because of his strong territorial claim, and although he loved chasing footballs, that day he totally ignored them. Bill and James wanted to film some slow-motion sequences, but when we finally succeeded in getting Christian to run or move, he stopped as soon as he heard the noisy slow-motion camera. Eventually, with no other alternative, we undid months of careful training by encouraging him to chase us. We were irresistible and

Christian could not believe his luck. Despite our torn clothing, the result was an enjoyable and worthwhile day's filming.

Several days later we saw the rushes of the first two days' filming. Christian looked beautiful, the slow-motion sequences of him running and playing were stunning, and none of us, not even Bill and Virginia, had seen a lion in slow motion before. For the first time we really appreciated the strength, the power, the perfect co-ordination.

This might have been Christian's last visit to the garden, because the Moravian minister, although extremely fond of him, had reluctantly told us that he could no longer exercise there. Other people had access to the garden, and could not now be expected to cope with Christian's boisterousness as we could. The day he had obstinately refused to get off the roof of the minister's car might also have been an influencing factor. But when we told him that we expected to be in Kenya in a few weeks' time, he kindly compromised by allowing us to come to the garden at 6:30 A.M. Naturally our lives had to be considerably readjusted. Christian, now finding his life at Sophisto-Cat increasingly monotonous needed his day broken by an afternoon outing, so the early morning exercise did not suit him either. Bill suggested building a compound for Christian at Leith Hill, so that the three of us could live there until we left for Kenya.

When the compound was completed, Christian left the King's Road and London for ever. Many of his World's End friends gathered to say good-bye. After living for several weeks under the strain of waiting for some unfortunate accident to happen, it was a relief to leave only pleasant memories behind. But we were sad. Our five very happy months with Christian at Sophisto-Cat had ended.

CHAPTER 7

Country Life

Bill and Virginia's house at Leith Hill is surrounded by an attractive, rambling garden, and although only thirty miles from London, it overlooks a valley of unspoiled countryside. When we arrived, their children and dogs were safely inside the house, and Christian had a taste of the freedom that awaited him in Africa. For the first time in his life he could do exactly what he wanted to do. He ran around the lawns, occasionally sniffing daffodils, and into the woods through the bluebells. It was a beautiful but incongruous setting for a lion. He continually came back to us, to show how happy he was.

It was necessary that Christian should live in the compound, but he was very pleased with it. It measured twenty-five yards by fifteen, and enclosed a huge tree, several shrubs and a colourful gipsy caravan. He was so excited that his first reaction was to climb the tree, but as he had never climbed one before, he was confused as to how to turn around and get down again. He just waited for us to help him. Bill thought that Christian would sleep under a shrub, but we suspected he would prefer to sleep in the caravan. We were to live in another caravan, near the compound. It was summer and the sun was shining and it was so peaceful in comparison with London.

That night we sold Christian. A contract had been drawn up between us and the film company making *The Lion at World's End*. The whole project would be an expensive one, and while it was unlikely we would not fully co-operate, we were required to relinquish to the company our ownership of Christian. But ownership of a lion is something intangible. Although animals can be physically bought and sold, you can never sell a relationship with one. Nevertheless we surrendered all legal control over Christian's future. We tried to view the transaction as a necessary formality, in his best interests, but we felt guilty and did not dare tell him. And we preferred to think of Christian becoming a Kenyan citizen, rather than the mere property of a film company.

Christian slept in the caravan of course. He greeted us effusively the next morning, relieved that we had not abandoned him and returned to London during the night. He seemed unruffled by his change of surroundings.

We expected to be at Leith Hill only a few weeks, but George was still having difficulty in finding an area that both he and the Kenyan Government found suitable, as the two he had suggested had not been approved. We were anxious to get Christian to Kenya, but we dreaded to think of how unattractive and desolate the district that finally met all the requirements might be. Always expecting to leave shortly, we waited while George continued searching, and the weeks passed. Fortunately it was summer and the weather was usually pleasant. We spent restful days reading, sunbathing, and playing with Christian. But as we are both basically city-orientated, one of us would occasionally go to London for a few days. Friends came down to visit the three of us.

Leith Hill became an important phase in Christian's life. He had fewer restrictions, and a less confusing, more clearly defined territory to live in. For the first time he experienced the natural cycle of a day. Sleeping in the caravan was a hangover from his life as a London lion. It was often hot, and he was lethargic during the day, but he became rather boisterous in the late afternoons and evenings. After living at Sophisto-Cat with Christian for five months and regularly putting him to bed at about 8:30 P.M., we discovered at Leith Hill that lions are naturally nocturnal! We spent most of our time in the compound, and he would look discontented if we were not with him. Yet he often ignored us once we were inside, for even if he did not want to play with us, as part of his pride, he just enjoyed the companionship. A double-gate system made entries and exits from the compound easy and safe.

Bill and Virginia have four young children and several dogs, and from his compound Christian watched their movements closely all the time. He would have loved to be included in their games. At Sophisto-Cat, if Christian had to be in the basement, he was ignorant of what he was missing upstairs. Lions do not like to be left out of anything, they like to have the freedom to decide if they want to participate. At Leith Hill a twelve-foot-high fence prevented Christian from joining in, but not from seeing, tempting games from which he was excluded. Unless we were with him, he frustratedly paced the fence, and very quickly wore a path along it. By now, it might have been a cage he was pacing in the same pointless, irrepressible way. After the initial mutual curiosity between Christian and the dogs, they lost interest in one another. But if one of the dogs strayed too close to the fence, Christian would tensely crouch and flatten his ears, imagining he was invisible. He sometimes forgot about his tail which swished in excitement. Then he would charge the fence and succeed in frightening away the dog, and because of the number of times he succeeded in stalking and almost knocking us to the ground, we felt his natural instincts had not been impaired.

Bill thought we could begin Christian's rehabilitation, in a small way, at Leith Hill. By comparisons we had made with other lions at Longleat, or at zoos, Christian was big for his age. But he needed to be as strong as possible for his introduction into his new life in Kenya. With constant exercise, and an outdoor life, he continued to grow rapidly and his body seemed more in proportion with his head and paws. He looked even healthier. On a rope from his tree we hung a sack

15. Virginia and the dogs

16. On the beach at West Wittering

17. With George Adamson in the compound at Nairobi airport

18. He enjoyed teasing the Africans with the safari company.

19.   The camp on the Tana River

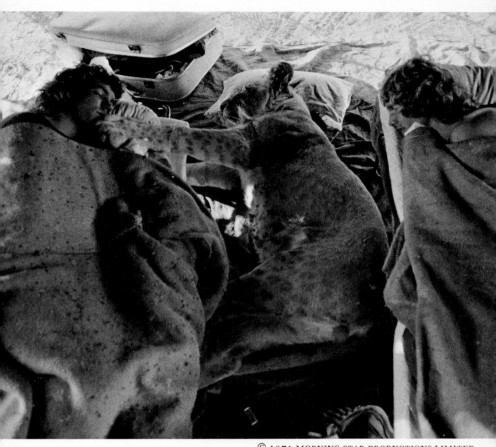

20.   His first night "in the wild"

21. "... a gesture of affection that could almost knock us to the ground."

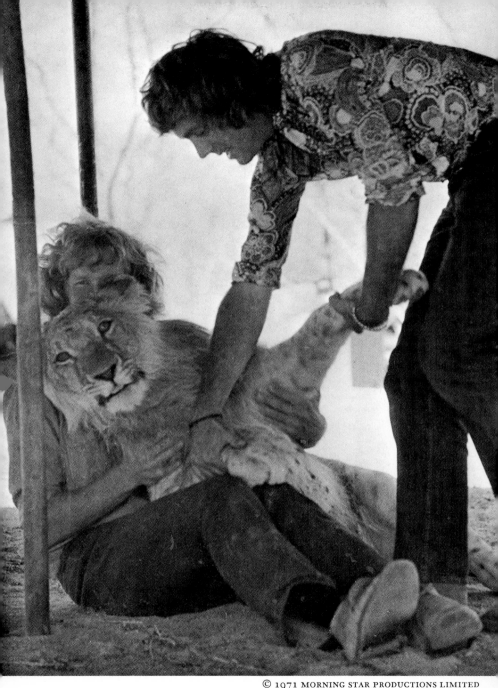

22.   In George's tent

23. The Tana River

24. The bush at Garissa

25. Christian would not be tempted into the water.

26.   Christian steps out in Africa.

27. George and Christian

28. Christian meets Katania.

29. Boy and Katania

30. George, Boy, and Katania

31. Boy angrily charged the wire each time Christian came too close.

32. Outside the wire, Boy repeatedly demanded submission from Christian.

filled with straw, and he adored attacking it, often swinging entirely off the ground. This was good practice for Kenya, and helped to develop useful muscles. He had learnt to keep his claws sheathed when we were playing with him; sharp, inch-long claws are an important weapon for a lion, and attacking the sack strengthened them, and taught him how to use them efficiently. Bill also changed Christian's diet. Lions in the wild usually kill in the evenings and have a varied diet. Christian was given a small milk and Farex meal in the morning and a large evening meal. In addition to raw meat, he had dried meat, carrots, cow livers and sometimes we gave him the head or stomach of a cow. His presence at Leith Hill had not been publicized, and the local butcher, mystified by our meat orders, asked, "What on earth are you two feeding, a crocodile?" As he knew we were living with Bill and Virginia, a lion would have been a more reasonable assumption.

His new diet improved his coat. It became thicker and softer, and was a beautiful lion-caramel colour. His partially-black mane became more pronounced, and he was growing into an extremely handsome lion. Perhaps inspired by the lower pollution level outside London, he spent more time keeping himself clean. His tongue was now so rough his licks on our faces could almost draw blood. He lost his milk teeth, and initiated his new ones by destroying several rungs of the ladder to his caravan.

He had more scope to express himself at Leith Hill, and because we had more time to appreciate him, our involvement with him grew closer. Unity came down from London several times each week to spend the day with him. New games were invented. He particularly enjoyed playing wheelbarrows with her, and became adept at tapping ankles and tripping people. He had a variety of toys, a new tyre, and several shrubs to play lions behind. He was content, and we found him irresistibly entertaining. Considering his size, he played extremely gently with us and remained easy to manage. It was perfectly safe for any of our visitors, other than children, to come into the compound with him. A lion prepared to play wheelbarrows, must have in addition to a sense of humour, a deep love for the human race.

But sometimes when it rained he grew quite wild, and then we stayed outside the compound. There was a difficult period when he became aware that he could easily prevent us from leaving the compound, by jumping up and holding us with his large front paws. Our smacks just made him more determined. Smacking a lion in a situation such as this required considerable audacity. But within a few days he realized that behaviour like this was self-defeating, for it meant we spent less time with him. He decided it was best to co-operate.

We had bought Christian when he was very young, and it had taken months for us to build up our understanding with him. We admired the tremendous courage Bill and Virginia had shown, playing their roles in *Born Free*, working with a cast of many adult lions, and with less opportunity to develop a similar relationship to ours with Christian. As he was soon to leave for Africa, it was pointless for Bill and Virginia to encourage a strong friendship with him, but they loved him, and came down to his compound several times each day to talk to him. When they were with him, because of their experience with lions, they handled him very well.

Christian's life at Leith Hill was filmed, with particular emphasis on the beginning of his rehabilitation. He had a strong affection for James Hill, and most of our time was spent preventing Christian from jumping on him. James insisted that he was not frightened, but just did not want to "have my new trousers torn." He seemed to have new trousers on each day we filmed, and he directed more comfortably from outside the compound.

Bill decided to take Christian, very early one morning, to his first English beach. We were not enthusiastic; 3 A.M. is an unappealing time to begin a day, and we knew that it would be us Christian would trample on during the sixty miles there and back. Christian was now too big to travel in a car so we went in Bill and Virginia's Dormobile, a motorized caravan. It was our first English beach as well, and it was grey, dismal, and deserted. But there was a beautiful dawn, and we filmed several sequences of Christian and the four of us running along the beach. He had no intention of getting wet. He enjoyed the outing, but finally tired of waiting on the leash each time until the cameras were positioned. It was unwise to irritate a lion of his size, so we took him home. His paw marks must have confused bathers later in the day.

He had now been at Leith Hill for ten weeks, and his life there had lost some of its attraction. And for us, our caravan seemed to diminish in size daily. Christian was becoming slightly frustrated, and part of the strain we had felt during his last weeks at Sophisto-Cat returned. He occasionally climbed the wire of his compound, and we hoped that this was just a way of attracting our attention, rather than an attempt to escape.

On 12 August 1970, Christian celebrated his first birthday. Unity made him a birthday cake out of fillet steak shaped with minced meat. It had one lighted candle on top, and before Christian blew it out and ate the cake, we made a wish that he would soon be in Kenya.

CHAPTER 8

Christian's Parents

We had to prepare Christian for his journey to Kenya, as it would be an ordeal. He was to fly by East African Airways, and regulations required him to travel in a crate in the pressurized hold. It was an eleven-hour flight, but because Christian would be put in his crate at Leith Hill, he faced at least fifteen hours' confinement. When Bill was making arrangements with the airline company, a representative said: "There seems to be a mistake, Mr. Travers. Surely you don't intend flying a lion from England to Africa, that's just taking coals to Newcastle."

We investigated the whole question of Christian's flight very thoroughly. We telephoned several animal dealers and zoos for information about the best methods of transporting animals. There was no agreement, or even interest, and it appears that animals are forced to travel with little regard for their well-being. Some of the people we spoke to suggested a small crate, in which it was impossible for the animal to turn around. The less room, the less scope the animal would have to move and injure himself. Bill spoke to Oliver Graham-Jones, who had been senior vet at the London Zoo, and was well known for arranging the transport of Chi-Chi the panda to Moscow and back. He advised that Christian should be mildly tranquillized by adding a sedative to his food, and said this would safely minimize any frustration. Christian would probably sleep for most of the journey. We decided to order a crate large enough for him to sit upright or turn around. It would have bars on one end and a sliding panel at the other. We specifically asked that there should be no rough surfaces or sharp edges on which he could injure himself.

The crate was delivered and for Christian to become familiar with it, we put it in his compound. He was fed in the crate, and we shut his caravan at night so he began to sleep in it too. Each day we shut him in for short periods, as practice, so that the actual journey would be less of a shock.

East African Airways quoted a charge of £2.00 per pound for flying Christian to Kenya, so we had to weigh him. We borrowed some scales from the even more mystified butcher, and tied them on to a rope from the tree. We put an empty sack under Christian's stomach, lifted him up, and slipped both ends of the sack on to the hook at the bottom of the scales. He dangled helplessly but good-naturedly. It had been an effort for Bill and us to lift him, and we were not surprised when we saw that he weighed 160 pounds. A veterinary certificate of health was also required, and Christian was examined by a vet, and inoculated with Catovac, as some form of protection from diseases he would have no immunity against in Africa.

We had always wanted to see Christian's parents at Ilfracombe Zoo in Devon, and because of the long delay at Leith Hill, we now had the opportunity to visit them. Butch and Mary were both three-year-olds, and the most magnificent lions we had ever seen. Christian looked very like his handsome, heavily-maned father. They were an affectionate couple, but incessantly paced around the cement floor of their cage. The owner of the zoo was prepared to sell them for £500, but we did not dare ask Bill if Butch and Mary could come to Kenya too.

We asked the owner about Christian's sisters. He told us the name of the animal dealer to whom he had sold them. We contacted him, but as he had sold fifty-eight lion cubs in 1969, and kept no detailed records, he could only say that he thought they had been sold to a circus. Christian's other sister at Harrods had been purchased by a man who found her too much of a responsibility, and disposed of her to a source he did not disclose. Ironically, many dogs and cats have pedigrees, yet it is almost impossible to trace a lion's history, as so few records are kept. Butch, who was purchased from the Rotterdam Zoo, may be related to Elsa, because Joy and George Adamson had sent Elsa's sisters to the Rotterdam Zoo from Kenya in 1956.

Christian's family history is depressingly typical of animals in captivity.

Inevitably we compared Christian's future with the life of his parents. Freedom, instead of cement, bars, and boredom. Neither of us had visited a zoo where animals were satisfactorily confined, and zoos should be constantly investigated, and certain standards maintained. We feel that being anti-zoo is unrealistic, since for the moment they have to be accepted as a fact of life. And in some, species such as the Arabian oryx, which are almost extinct in their natural state, have been temporarily saved. Christian had awakened in us a general feeling of responsibility towards all other animals. Bill and Virginia both said that their association with the lions during the filming of *Born Free* had had an enormous influence on their lives. We frequently discussed with them the whole question of the conservation and protection of wild animals and we realized, for the first time, how drastically short-sighted man has been.

Sitting in our caravan at Leith Hill we decided to create the best zoo in the world. For convenience, and because he was the inspiration behind our concept, we called our zoo, at the risk of sounding like a discothéque, Christian's. Our zoo would be an example to all others, provide the best possible living conditions in captivity, and make accessible the best and most up-to-date information about animal life.

We would give world experts the chance to create the best conditions for animals in captivity, and they would work in conjunction with leading architects and designers. The restrictions would be of the most sensitive and sophisticated nature. In addition to our perfectly exhibited, healthier and happier animals, we would provide halls where zoologists lectured, and cinemas to show films like *Born Free,* and documentaries about animals in their natural state. We would have bookshops, and a library of books and films. Our zoo would become a centre of research and information, providing standards and advice on the conservation and care of animals in captivity, for people all over the world.

To us, in our caravan, it appeared a totally feasible project. Since we are unable to finance it ourselves, our idea should, because of increasing awareness of animal conservation, attract financial support and be assisted by the government. It would require a considerable area of land, yet, as the public are so obviously prepared to go "to Africa and back in a day" at Longleat, 100 miles from London, we could assume they would come to Christian's.

We began to think how we could have designed a compound for Christian that would have resulted in his feeling less restricted. Why do animals in zoos have to live in compounds and cages which have such monotonous symmetry, no variety, and no evidence of any imagination in their design? Why not have compounds where humans walk by an enclosed corridor into the centre, and the animals would have the freedom to walk almost entirely around the humans. There would be at least some transference of the feeling of restriction.

We waited at Leith Hill for so long that Christian outgrew his crate. We noticed that when he was shut in, he sometimes frustratedly pawed the vertical bars, and rubbed his pads quite raw. For his next, larger crate, we requested that the bars be placed horizontally, which would make it impossible for him to injure himself in this way. Although it had been supplying zoos and animal dealers for many years, the company which made the crates had never been asked to make this, to us very obvious, improvement. This seemed indicative of how retarded our thinking about animals is.

After three months at Leith Hill, we began to despair that George would ever find a suitable site for Christian's rehabilitation. But then a cable arrived from Kenya. Christian would be leaving England in a few days.

CHAPTER 9

"Coals to Newcastle"

At 3:30 P.M. on 22 August 1970, Christian was led into his crate, not for the customary few minutes, but for at least fifteen hours. Pouring rain was his last memory of England. In pieces of meat he was fed the tranquillizers, and then the crate was carried to the van which was to take him to London's Heathrow Airport. Lions have no luggage, and we could leave his leash behind, as there would be no further use for it. Unity had of course come to Leith Hill to say good-bye to him, and with tears in her eyes, she promised to visit him in Kenya.

Following Bill and Virginia in their car, we travelled to the airport in the van with Christian, who was confused but not alarmed. The car with our cameraman was stopped by the police for filming without a permit, also for cutting across traffic and causing an obstruction. But the combination of Virginia McKenna and a lion on his way to Africa persuaded the surprised policeman to be lenient, and the convoy was allowed to proceed. At Heathrow we drove out on to the tarmac and parked beside the aeroplane. Hessian was tied around the crate, as insulation against the cold on the long night flight. The tranquillizers were effective, for Christian was quite relaxed, despite the noise from other aircraft and the curious crowd that gathered. At 5:30 P.M., after Virginia had said good-bye to him, Christian was fork-lifted into the small pressurized hold of the aeroplane. It was a dramatic but not a happy moment, for we all realized there was a possibility that in the hold, amongst the luggage, Christian could die.

We left England at 7:00 P.M. with Bill and the film crew, and with Christian somewhere underneath us. The only scheduled stop, before Nairobi Airport in Kenya, was at Paris one hour later. There we were allowed to climb into the hold, where to our immense relief we found Christian sleepy and calm. Bill decided that it was unnecessary to give him more tranquillizers, so we just slipped pieces of meat through the bars to him and refilled his water bowl. But the most demanding, longest part of the flight still lay ahead.

We landed at Nairobi Airport at 7:00 A.M. Uninterrupted sunshine is assumed in Africa, as it is in Australia, but it was overcast and cold, and we realized it was winter. Christian's crate was unloaded. He had survived and his ordeal was over, but no longer tranquillized, he was very agitated. George Adamson was there to meet us, and he arranged for Christian to be wheeled off to an animal-holding compound, where he waited while we went through Immigration and Customs. Christian was relieved to be let out of his crate, and greeted us affectionately. George described him as "a handsome, friendly little fellow." Though he was uninjured and unmarked, Christian walked unsteadily and looked totally exhausted. His eyes were bleary, his coat had lost condition, and he seemed thinner. But at last he was in Kenya.

The area allotted by the Kenyan Government for his rehabilitation, was near Garissa, 280 miles northeast of Nairobi. To reach it, the last twenty miles had to be cut by George's brother, Terence Adamson, and an African labour force. The track was now nearly cleared and Bill and George decided to make the journey in two stages, so as to provide sufficient time for the hired safari company to prepare our camp at Garissa. It would also be easier for Christian.

Garissa had been chosen basically because no one else wanted it. George described it as a desolate, unattractive part of Kenya. No Africans live there, it has tsetse flies, and in the wet season it is inaccessible. The game, while not abundant, would be adequate for Christian and the other lions in the pride that George intended to form. For the exclusive use of this unwanted land the film company had to pay £750 a year.

Christian remained in the holding-compound at the airport for two days. We stayed in Nairobi, and several times each day drove out to see and feed him. He was content to sleep if we were not there. Our visits attracted enormous crowds of Africans and we realized that most of them had never seen a lion, or many other indigenous animals. Until recently, only tourists could afford to visit the Game Parks. Each time Christian walked towards the gate of the compound, the crowd stepped back apprehensively. Talking to various officials at the airport, we discovered that they could not grasp the point of rehabilitation, or why Christian had been flown from England at such expense.

We visited the Nairobi National Park and it was exciting to see so many animals in their natural environment, although we were only fifteen miles from Nairobi and the Hilton Hotel was clearly visible on the horizon. Bill had the opportunity to show George and several other people the rough cut of the English sequences in the film, and George was particularly interested to see a lion filmed in slow motion for the first time.

Within two days Christian had fully recovered from his flight. Early next morning we left Nairobi, in several Land-Rovers, for the first stage of the journey. Christian travelled in the back of George's Land-Rover, and to our concern, he paced relentlessly and quickly rubbed bare patches on his nose and forehead, on the wire barrier between him and the front seats. We stopped frequently to give him water and to try and pacify him, and George probably thought that we were unnecessarily worried about our pampered lion.

We were interested in our first drive through Kenya, but as the day progressed it became increasingly hotter, drier and more desolate. We had been depressed by

George's description of Garissa, and now we could see for ourselves the country that Christian was to live in. We drove 200 miles, and just before nightfall arrived at a temporary camp prepared by the safari company where we were to spend two nights. Christian was exhausted and we led him into a small compound. We decided to put our beds in with him, and he promptly got on to one of them and fell asleep. His first night in the wild.

In the stillness and refreshing coolness of the African evening, we sat down to a superbly set table, and Africans in flowing blue kaftans and red boleros and caps served us a delicious three-course meal. It was a ridiculous but pleasant surprise. We asked George about the other lions that were to be rehabilitated with Christian. For his man-made pride George already had two others waiting at Naivasha, and in a few days he would have to return to collect them. One was Katania, a four-month-old lioness, who had been found and given to George, her mother being presumed dead. The other was Boy, a seven-year-old lion who had been used in the filming of *Born Free,* and one of those George had been allowed to rehabilitate in 1965. The rehabilitation had been successful, but one day Joy Adamson had, quite by chance, found Boy badly injured, perhaps by a buffalo. He was operated on by Dr. Tony Harthoorn and his wife Sue, and during the complicated operation they inserted a steel pin into one of Boy's legs. Joy and George Adamson nursed him for nine months at Naivasha. It was a fortunate coincidence that Bill had contacted George about Christian at the time when Boy was almost well enough to be released again.

Next morning Christian had his first walk in Africa. We symbolically took off his collar, now to be permanently discarded, and followed him with Bill and George. The country was barren and totally featureless, and Christian, who had appeared so big in a London furniture shop, was suddenly dwarfed by his surroundings. It was extremely hot, and he just walked quietly, absorbing everything. Instinctively he knew how to remove thorns from his paws, with his teeth, and we saw that the colour of his coat was a natural camouflage. He was so obviously in his rightful setting.

Since it was a waterless region, it was unlikely that we would see any other animals. But late that afternoon a gombi, a large African cow, came wandering towards the camp. Separated from its herd, it was looking for water or food. Christian saw the gombi, and immediately began to stalk it. The animal had enormous sharp horns, and George told us to stop Christian, for as he was so inexperienced he could easily be injured. But he would not be restrained. George raced to his Land-Rover and drove between Christian and the gombi which then ran off. Before Christian could follow it, we both grabbed him to put him in the Land-Rover. But for the second time in his life he snarled a terrifying warning, and we instantly released him. The gombi had disappeared and Christian, justifiably angry, reluctantly followed us back to camp.

George was impressed by Christian's perfect, instinctive stalking of the gombi, and explained to us how he had fanned out in a wide semicircle, using the natural cover of the bushes. He had been correctly positioned so that the wind would not carry his scent to the gombi, and alert it. George said, "We won't have any trouble adapting young Christian to the wild," and we were very proud of him.

It was now eighty miles to our final camp near Garissa. But the road was rough and covered with powdery volcanic dust, and we had to drive very slowly. To our relief, as we drew closer to the camp which was on the Tana River, the countryside became slightly more fertile and varied. Amongst other animals we saw an elephant and some giraffes, and Africa began to come alive. We drove past a village whose inhabitants were tall, graceful people, wearing simple robes and fantastic necklaces and bracelets. They were the first Africans we had seen apparently living as they have for centuries, and not wearing drab Western clothes.

For the last twenty miles it was often necessary to use the four-wheel drive on the Land-Rovers, particularly when crossing sandy river beds. Cutting the track had been an enormous task, and it was obvious why the area was inaccessible in the wet season. We arrived late in the the afternoon to find the camp was in an unexpectedly beautiful setting. Our tents were amongst the dom palms, beside the wide Tana River. The long journey was over.

George left the next morning to collect his other lions from Naivasha, and was away for several days. We were thoroughly spoiled; our tents were comfortable and insect-free, our meals were prepared, hot showers were available and our clothes were washed and somehow ironed. Christian had a compound near the tents to sleep in at night. However the Africans with the safari company were terrified of him, and if he teased them too often we had to keep him in the compound during the day too. Because of the heat, we were all lethargic. Christian behaved like the worst English tourist, avoiding the sun, and lolling on our camp-beds at every opportunity, probably dreaming of London.

In the early mornings before it became too hot, or in the late afternoons, we went for walks with Christian. We shall never forget this freedom of just walking with him, after the eight months in England so full of the restrictions we had had to impose. He would bossily push his way in front of us, and always insist on leading. But he was easy to direct, and showed no inclination to wander off by himself. Fortunately on these walks we did not meet any other animals, for we knew we would not be able to restrain him. If we went for a swim, he sat in the shade and watched. He was fascinated by the baboons barking at him from across the river, and the hippopotami that occasionally surfaced. No doubt he also saw the crocodiles that ominously slid into the water whenever we appeared. We swam briefly.

In several ways Christian seemed very much a beginner, with a lot to learn. He was inept at climbing rocks, and we often had to show him the way or help him. For the first time in his life he was not wholly dependent on us for amusement, but we were slightly concerned by his lack of interest in investigating anything by himself. There were many thorn bushes, and although he was able to pull the thorns out of the pads of his paws, he often just looked helpless and waited for us to do it. His pads were tender, and because of the long walks and the thorns they became quite raw. But already they were toughening.

He was content and free, and very gentle with us. Although now a large animal, he would sometimes spontaneously leap into our arms, a gesture of affection that could almost knock us to the ground. And soon, other lions would arrive to make his happiness complete.

CHAPTER 10

A Lion's Lion

W hile George went to Naivasha to collect Boy and Katania, and we stayed by the river, Terence Adamson was building another camp for George, in much less attractive surroundings, several miles from the Tana River. This was to discourage the lions from swimming across the crocodile-infested river to the other side which was a Hunting Block, where there was a danger that the lions could be shot. George intended to live there for at least two years, which would give him time to form a full pride, and the lions the chance to establish their territory and operate independently. This second camp was more permanent, with several huts and tents within two large wire compounds.

Boy and Katania arrived at Garissa, and were taken to George's camp. In two days they both had recovered from their long journey, and it was time for Christian to be introduced to his first lions. The initial test in his rehabilitation was that he should be able to assimilate into a life with other lions, and had not been retarded by his eight months among humans. George knew that the introduction would have to be a gradual one, spread perhaps over weeks. He wanted to live with Christian in one compound, separated by a strong, high wire fence from Boy and Katania in the other compound. Living side by side, they would develop a familiarity, and eventually they could be fully introduced. As in all relationships, human or animal, compatibility cannot be assumed, especially in this case, when the backgrounds of Boy and Christian were at such variance. Unsure of what would happen, excited but apprehensive, we drove innocent Christian up to George's camp. He followed us into the first compound, and in the other one we saw Katania and Boy. Katania was tiny, and our attention was riveted to Boy. He was enormous, impressive, and stood motionless, his eyes on Christian, who was instantly aware of his presence, but unwilling even to look at him, and understandably confused and frightened. We walked to Bill and George, who were standing a few yards from the dividing wire fence. Christian was reluctant to follow, but slowly picked his way towards us, his eyes averted from Boy. Bewildered, he crouched behind us, pressed against our legs. Katania sensed the impending events and wisely kept well away. Suddenly, with a dreadful roar, Boy ferociously charged at Christian. Under his weight the wire gave slightly, and we all scattered. Poor Christian remained where he was, but cringed and snarled. Momentarily satisfied, Boy walked away. Christian was badly shaken and needed consoling. He was affectionate, and by sitting on us, insisted that we did not leave him. It was a shock for him to discover that he was not the only lion in the world, and worse, that the first one he met was three times his size. We waited a few yards from the wire for about half an hour. Boy kept a nonchalant eye on Christian, who either sat on us, or hid behind our legs pretending to be asleep. Several times he charged at Christian, who again cowered and snarled.

We moved away from the wire, the intial introduction was over. Boy had behaved predictably, for as an adult lion he demanded submission from Christian. Christian was very nervous all day, and although his eyes were constantly on Boy, he stayed close to us, well away from the wire. That night we put a bed for him between our beds, but our sleep was broken by Boy's powerful, haunting roars, which frightened Christian and us equally.

Christian spent most of the next day on George's bed, although he was free to leave the compound if he wished. We were rather worried about him, he seemed at home on the bed, taking no interest in Boy or Katania. He occasionally gave them a cool glance in the next compound. But late in the afternoon he walked to within a few yards of the dividing fence. Katania came over and really rather flirted with him. Christian was interested but did not move any closer. Boy charged towards him and again Christian cowered. He then casually retreated and came back to us, but he had made a positive step.

The following morning George constructed a small hatch between the two compounds so that Katania could be with either Boy or Christian. The crucial introduction would be between Boy and Christian, but Katania could be a helpful link. She tentatively came through the hatch twice, but Christian was of course asleep on a bed, and did not see her. Again we were concerned about Christian's lack of interest in communicating with them. He pretended they did not exist, but we sensed that, when awake, he knew exactly what their movements were.

Later we took him for a walk, and he seemed relieved to be away from Boy and Katania. The countryside stretched endlessly, broken only occasionally by outcrops of rock. It was unattractive in comparison with the camp site beside the Tana River, but still rather beautiful. Various shades of grey and brown, and splashes of green around dried-up water holes. Barren, and covered by low, thick thorn bushes, it was a harsh area for the lions to live in. Christian had come to what could be described as another World's End.

Back in the camp he teased the Africans constructing the huts; he bit a few bottoms and kneecaps, and jumped on whatever they happened to be carrying. These Africans adjusted to Christian, but were always wary of him. George was interested to see that Christian, unlike most other lions, showed no colour distinction. Boy, who will accept Europeans, growled fiercely each time an African came too close to his compound but Christian did not share this dislike, and he amused us all for the afternoon. He seemed a travesty of a lion.

Christian, in high spirits, then became rather provocative with Boy. We noticed that he focused his attention almost entirely on him. Christian strode boldly up to the dividing wire and lay down. Boy charged and Christian turned and fled. But he came back a few minutes later and appeared to be teasing Boy, who was outraged by this impudence and charged angrily. Christian even poked his head through Katania's hatch, but hastily withdrew it when Boy spotted him. Perhaps he had tired of having no contact with them, yet strangely it still seemed more natural for Christian to be with humans rather than lions. We certainly appeared to appreciate him more.

The next day George decided that it was time for Christian to meet Katania, who had been unwilling to leave Boy and come through the hatch to Christian. It was unusual for a fully grown lion and a four-month-old lioness to have such a strong, affectionate relationship. In a natural pride the adult lion has little contact with the cubs. But since they had been brought together at Naivasha, Boy, to his embarrassment, had been cast in the role of mother-substitute.

George led Boy out of his compound, and Christian stalked him as he walked past. Boy rushed at the fence, but his charges now seemed less convincing, and we suspected that he was rapidly becoming bored with this necessary display of authority. Interestingly, when he charged this time, Christian snarled as usual, but for the first time rolled over on his back, the gesture of submission from the younger lion that Boy demanded.

With Boy outside we could then take Christian

through a gate into the other compound. He walked up to the other end, where Katania was pacing, distressed by her separation from Boy. Christian approached her confidently, and they exchanged a beautiful greeting, their heads gently touching. He was intrigued, and continually licked and smelt her. Boy jealously watched all this from the outside, but after an initial charge at the fence to separate them, he appeared resigned.

Christian and Katania played together, and although he was much bigger, he was very gentle, and she squealed on the few occasions he was too rough with her. He followed her, tapping her back legs and tripping her. This was a game that he and Unity had devised at Leith Hill. Christian was delighted to have a lion to play with, and afterwards we thought that he was rather smug and off-hand with us!

Boy was led back into the other compound, and Katania ran through the hatch to greet him. After smelling her, he grimaced to show his displeasure at Christian's scent, but another step had been taken. We were uneasy about Boy's spending the night with us, as we had not been introduced to him either. To our horror he chose to sleep in our tent, and we did not dare argue.

On the following day George thought that enough time had elapsed for Christian to be safely introduced to Boy. It was a meeting we had all waited for anxiously, but aware that if there was a fight between them, Christian had no chance. The decision was George's and we relied on his experience. We led Christian up on to a large flat rock where he wanted them to meet.

Then Bill and George led Boy and Katania to the rock from a different direction. Boy and Katania lay down about fifteen yards from Christian, who was watching intently. For twenty minutes we stood nervously and watched the three lions. Although impatient to make contact with Boy, Christian sensed that it was not for him to make the first move.

Katania became bored with the tense situation and wandered towards Christian, and they greeted one another. Boy immediately stood up and charged at Christian. It was a frightening moment, intensified by their roars and snarls. Christian rolled over on his back submissively, and, satisfied, Boy lay down a few yards from him. Although they appeared to be fighting, very little physical contact had been made, and Christian seemed to be unhurt.

After an interval of about ten minutes, Katania, who had wisely run off during the last encounter, again came over to Christian, and triggered off a repeat performance. This time Boy walked away, leaving Christian badly shaken and looking miserable. He came over to us, and, comforting him, we walked back to camp.

Although it was a man-made situation, we had witnessed a natural introduction between an adult lion and a younger, strange lion. Despite our feelings for Christian, we felt intruders in an animal society. Christian had instinctively known what his role was, and he had obeyed the conventions of the lion world by his submission. George commented that Christian, by his determination to face Boy, and not fleeing from him, had shown considerable courage. Christian was fond of Katania, but it was Boy's acceptance he was so anxious to win. To gain this, he had to endure some unpleasant but necessary formalities.

We could now all live in the same compound. Over the next few days, Christian stayed as close to Boy as he would permit. If Christian was too daring, Boy would charge, but the charges had lost their intensity. With adoration Christian concentrated solely on Boy, and even imitated his movements; he followed him around, sat down when he sat down, and lay in the same position. We often saw him lying just around a corner from Boy, a clever trick to get closer to him than would normally be allowed. He sometimes played with Katania, but like us, she was a poor second. Christian was still affectionate towards us, but he was definitely a lion's lion.

Each morning George went out walking with the lions, until they chose some shade in which to spend the hottest hours of the day. Christian followed behind Boy and Katania, but sat down and looked in another direction whenever Boy noticed him. In the afternoons we would find the three lions together, but Christian was always a few yards away. With them, but not yet part of them.

We had an extraordinary human–animal co-existence living with the lions at Garissa. We spent ridiculous nights, often with the three of them in our tent. While Katania bit our toes or stole our blankets, Christian hid under a bed, and Boy just roared.

After a few days Boy greeted us in the way he greeted Bill and George. His huge head would rub up against us. He had a placid nature, but a total assumption of superiority. He did only what pleased him. Filming had continued at Garissa, and we often had to wait hours until Boy was suitably positioned. In contrast, we just carried Christian into the correct position, or simply rolled him over to face the cameras. We found ourselves describing Boy as a "marvellous" lion, and physically he was, but compared with Christian he had little personality. Our praise of him was basically motivated by our relief that he had eaten neither us nor Christian.

Christian had now been in Africa for several weeks and he was tougher. His pads had hardened, and his coat had become sleeker and slightly darker. He was growing into a very handsome lion, and Bill described him as the "Jean-Paul Belmondo of the lion world." He had always been healthy, but one day he was suddenly listless. We thought he might be depressed by Boy's reluctance to fully accept him. But because of the whiteness of his gums, and his hot nose, George took his temperature and diagnosed tick fever. Christian had no immunity against this disease, and George fortunately anticipating it, was able to inject him with the appropriate vaccine. He believes that Elsa died from tick fever, and had he had this vaccine then, he might have saved her. Christian was very sick for two days, but he quickly recovered.

Now that Christian had been introduced to Boy, Bill and the film crew could return to England, with their film complete. George suggested that we should also leave Garissa for a short time, to give Christian the chance to adjust to our no longer being part of his life. We decided to visit other parts of Kenya and Tanzania, before returning to see Christian for the last time.

CHAPTER 11

Onward Christian

On the route we followed through Kenya and Tanzania, we saw a variety of animals, in often spectacular surroundings. We were most impressed by the dramatically beautiful Ngorongoro Crater, and there we saw our first wild lions, three cubs and two lionesses. But there was something disturbingly unnatural about "wild" lions who were unconcerned by the Land-Rovers that totally encircled them, and tourists leaning out of the windows taking photographs. We were amused by the spirit of the woman at the Amboseli Game Reserve who had been driven by a guide to see the unusual sight of a lion guarding his freshly killed buffalo from vultures. "I've come to see the kills," she said, "not carcasses. Drive on."

Conditions in the lodges where we stayed varied from

nights under canvas, to the luxurious. All the lodges were expensive, and full of enthusiastic middle-aged tourists, who seemed to feel that the cost of their African holiday was justified if they saw one lion. Having flown with our own lion to Africa, we were less easily satisfied. We had been spoiled by our weeks at Garissa, living with several lions, and at a level and pace at which it was possible to absorb a real feeling for Africa. Rather than have many animals paraded before us, we preferred to see a few of them unexpectedly, or by waiting motionless at the Tana River for hours, watching them warily come for their evening drink.

We went to see Joy Adamson at Lake Naivasha, who was anxious to hear news of the lions. She was relieved that Boy's leg appeared to have fully recovered although he still walked with a faint limp. We spent several hours with her talking about animals, particularly lions and cheetahs, and her ideas about wild-life conservation in Australia. She was curious about Christian's background and his life in England with us, and hoped to visit him soon.

On our way through Nairobi, we took a sample of Christian's blood to the vets, Tony and Sue Harthoorn. George had correctly diagnosed tick fever, and they told us that there was a slight chance that it would recur, but George had the correct vaccine to combat it. Boy and Katania were also susceptible to this disease, just by having moved from one part of Kenya to another.

On the long drive back we lost our way in the darkness, and were alarmed when our Land-Rover was flagged down by what looked like almost naked, spear-

holding warriors. We thought we should stop, but quickly
wound up the windows. We then realized they were
embarrassingly young African children with sticks,
merely wanting cigarettes. In English, they directed us to
Garissa!

We arrived at George's camp late that night. He was
concerned about Christian who for the first time had
not returned with Boy and Katania in the evening.
George had looked for him and called him, but he had
not appeared.

However, within several minutes of our arrival, Christian came running towards the camp. We had been
away for a fortnight and, wildly excited, he leapt all over
us. George believed he must have had a premonition
we were returning and thinks lions have a sixth sense
that humans either have lost, or never had. On visits
to his other lions after their release in the wild he
has often arrived in a deserted camp only to be joined
by them a few minutes later, although they could not
have known he was coming.

Christian had obviously missed us. He made con-
tinuous happy grunts while leaping on us and licking our
faces. When we sat down, he would clamber on to one
our laps, then stretch across to have at least part of his
body, his front paws, on the other one. He excitedly
jumped on the table, creating chaos, and making eating
impossible. He did not allow us to sleep.

We were delighted to see that he looked well, and that
George was fond of him, and found him as amusing
as we did. One night George had unwisely made Christian a snack of powdered milk, a great favourite from

his English days. And now, every night, Christian followed him around, tapping his ankles and butting him with his head, until he relented and gave him his powdered milk.

Boy had still not fully accepted Christian. There had been an improvement, but apparently Christian sometimes became depressed by his unrequited adoration of Boy. He and Katania were now very friendly, and George thought that it might be Boy's jealousy that was prolonging the present tension.

He told us of an incident which had happened the day we left Garissa. He had followed the lions on their morning walk, and quite close to the camp he had seen an enormous rhinoceros. Boy and Katania tactfully moved well away from it. But to George's alarm, Christian began to walk towards the rhinoceros. He stalked it perfectly, and came to within a few yards, when the rhinoceros suddenly turned and saw him and, snorting with rage at Christian's impudence, he charged. Christian sprang eight feet in the air, over a bush, and fled. George was most amused, but hoped Christian had learnt his lesson.

Already Boy had spent several nights away in an attempt to establish a territory. He chose the opposite side of the camp from the direction in which we had heard a wild lion roaring on several occasions. However, it was impossible for a single fully grown lion to establish a territory alone and George told us he planned to bring two other lions up to the camp. He had found a lion and a lioness of about Christian's age who had been captured after they had frequently attacked domestic cattle and who, but for George's intervention, would have been destroyed.

This time we spent only a few days with George and Christian. Each morning we walked with the lions until they chose a tree or bush under which to shelter from the sun, Christian always accompanied Boy and Katania, but Boy suffered his presence rather than encouraged it. In the afternoons we walked with George to find them, fascinated by the way he could follow their spoor. The lions returned in the evenings to be fed, and George had to drive many miles to a Hunting Block, to shoot water buck or other game for them to eat. He hoped they would soon be self-sufficient.

We loved talking to George and had long conversations with him, not only about lions, but also about Australia and our lives in London. Although he has often led an isolated life, George has kept in touch with events in the outside world. Since he had been to school in England, but had returned only once, he was interested to hear how London had changed, and what its attraction was for people like us.

He talked to us of his early days as a hunter and how, when he realized the danger of extinction that faced many animals, he became increasingly concerned for their conservation. Since Elsa's death he has devoted his life to experimenting with the rehabilitation of lions. With Bill and Virginia's help, Christian had been delivered into the most sympathetic and knowledgeable person in the world.

George loves lions, and believes it is possible to attain an understanding with them that is less likely, if not impossible, with other animals. He admires their dignity and their immense capacity for love and trust. He is happy to live with them at Garissa, until they are no longer dependent on him.

He felt that Boy was about to grant Christian the acceptance he longed for, and other lions, in addition to easing the situation, would complete the nucleus of a pride that Christian would be a part of. He was confident that the rehabilitation of all the lions would be successful.

Christian now had the freedom to take his chance in the wild, and we decided not to prolong the departure we had both been dreading. Life would be empty without him. Sitting by the river with Christian on our last afternoon, our sadness was tempered by the peace and beauty of Africa. We watched the spectacular red and orange sunset that would end each day for him. Christian, after a journey of several generations, and thousands of miles, had returned to where he belonged.

Postscript

Several months after we left Garissa, we had news of Christian, Boy, and Katania in a letter from George Adamson, part of which follows:

> If you have been in touch with Bill recently, I expect you have heard about the tragedy of poor little Katania. One evening last month the three lions pushed off towards the river after having a good feed of meat. They did not return the following morning, which was nothing unusual, as on several occasions they had been absent for two or three days, once even for five days. I went searching for them two days later but without success. In the early hours of the next day Christian appeared alone. This was a little worrying as usually he and Katania kept to-

gether, while Boy went off looking for girls. However, I thought Katania must surely be with Boy. Early next morning Boy arrived, alone.

Now there was real cause for alarm, and Christian seemed just as worried as I was. I started an intensive search on foot and by Land-Rover. I took Christian walking with me, relying on his powers of scent for help. It was not until four days later that I found the spoor of the three lions on the bank of the river, about three miles below where you stayed by the Tana before moving up to my camp. It was plain to see that Christian and Katania had been playing, racing up and down along the bank. I crossed to the far bank but found Boy's tracks only. On the near side, there were only the tracks of Christian leaving the river, I think Katania must have tried to follow Boy into the water, but being so much lighter and smaller, was carried down by the current, and before she could make the bank, she was taken by a crocodile. Even at her age lions are very good swimmers, and it is unlikely that she would have drowned. It is a sad loss which I feel keenly, as do Boy and Christian. The joy has gone out of them.

About a fortnight ago, Boy went off on another foray across the river and returned with a girlfriend. I could hear them around the camp for three days and nights. One night while Boy was busy with his lioness, I heard Christian growling near the edge of the bush in front of the camp. By the light of a torch, I saw him facing another wild lioness of about his own age.

Boy and Christian are now good friends. In fact, Boy often takes the initiative in the greeting ritual of mutual head rubbing. Christian has started to accompany Boy in his roaring! A trifle immature, but a darned good effort. His voice promises to be even deeper than Boy's. A few days ago, there is reason to think that the two met up with the lionesses again, who may have made a kill, as both returned looking well fed and not in the least hungry after three days.

I soon hope to collect the lion and lioness that you know about. From the description given to me, I would say they are about fourteen months old, which means that they should have already had experience of hunting with their mother. They should be a big asset, provided I can gain their trust and friendship.

Bill Travers flew out to Kenya shortly after we received this news from George, and this is the letter Bill wrote to us on his return to England:

Dear John and Anthony,

I arrived back from Africa at the week-end. I can imagine your concern over the past weeks and thirst for news of Christian, so before I go into details of how he is making out, let me tell you first of all that he is both alive and well. He does not seem to have had a day's sickness since the tick fever he had when you were both out there. And he is very much alive I can assure you—my pawmarked khaki trousers will bear witness to that. He is a good deal heavier too, well over 200 lbs I would say at a guess, though sometimes when he greeted me fondly it felt considerably more. I am quite sure we could never now lift and suspend him from the local butcher's scales as we once did in England to find out his exact weight for the flight to Kenya, even if he would still allow it. He is as high at the shoulder as any fully grown lion, even as tall as Boy who, as you know, is a big lion. But in spite of his size he is as affectionate as ever. He gives George long ceremonial greetings with his head, licks him with his sandpaper tongue the moment George puts a foot outside the wire fencing that runs round the camp, inside which Christian is now no longer allowed.

However, this affection does not seem to be hampering the progress of rehabilitation, but in a strange way gives George the control that he will continue to need during the months that it takes to establish the lions first as a family and then as guardians of their territory.

By the way, I noticed that his coat seems to have adjusted to the hotter climate and is thinner, much finer and smoother, which makes him look more streamlined, more mature and certainly emphasises his now fine athletic figure. He is really quite a magnificent lion, and it would be hard to find anything to criticise in his appearance, except perhaps his feet. They are still enormous. I can only think if he grows big enough to make them look normal he will be, without doubt, the biggest lion in Africa.

After you left Boy and Christian became the greatest of friends—in fact quite inseparable, and the little cub Katania, who as you saw adored them both, found herself as they flopped over each other, the protesting centre of a sandwich.

Unfortunately, this friendship, as you have already been told, was short-lived. I won't therefore dwell on the circumstances which led us to assume the death of Katania, except to say it was doubly tragic. Not only had Boy and Christian lost their little friend, we'd also lost the only female in George's pride.

However, there is good news too, to compensate. The two lions George has collected are about the right age for Christian—a few months younger than he is. Unlike Christian they are already quite wild, and though too young to kill must have learned from their parents how to hunt. They must also have some knowledge of the strict rules of lion society. I think Christian will benefit greatly from his association with them as the pavements of Chelsea and the soft country life at our home were hardly the best schooling for the life he is now starting to lead. The other good part of this news is that one of them is a female. George, of course, is delighted as it is essential to have at least one female in the family or pride which we hope eventually will be able, with George's help, to establish itself in the Tana River area and enjoy freedom and a natural expression of life.

Well, I am sure there can hardly be a day that you do not talk or at least think about Christian, George and Boy. I can only tell you that the last picture I took with me, as I drove away from George's camp, was one of the three friends standing happily together for a final word outside the gate of their "home." A pat, a handshake, and they remained watching my Land-Rover as it started bumping down the long trail back to Nairobi and civilisation. I looked back as often as I dared take my eyes off the road and saw Christian rub against George, who fondled his slight mane, then wander off to Boy, to greet, nudge and no doubt provoke him into starting some wonderful sprawling lion game.

I felt strangely happy. I think if it were not for George Adamson and for people such as yourselves, Christian would have ended up in very different circumstances. . . .

All the best,
Yours,
Bill